BRAVE
Women of the Bible

The **Extraordinary** *Bravery*
of an **Ordinary** *Life*

by Faith Ann Raider

Contents

This is an invitation...

To something that might feel new. It's an invitation to discover a life lifed freely, lightly, and openly - an invitation to embrace the bravery God offers us right here in the middle of our everyday, ordinary lives; In the middle of the noise and the chaos, heartache and uncertainty that we find ourselves in; in our abundance, and in our emptiness, in the noise, and in the quiet, with our words, and with our silence, in our busyness, and in our stillness.

I see my friends - face-to-face and on social media - struggling, just like I do. Some of us are in a season of intense pain, and some of us are just weighed down with the junk and mess of ordinary life. Mostly, I think we are experiencing a little bit of both. We are feeling crushed by the pressure-cooker of life, trying to navigate our long, lonely wildernesses and our fiery trials, and feeling like we are just hanging on by a thread.

We all have places in our lives where we have the opportunity to embrace this bravery, moment-by-moment, day-by-day. I am learning that sometimes the bravest thing I can do is surrender every last one of my expectations and trust God, no matter what I'm seeing or how I'm feeling. Other days it is embracing the reality of needing others and being honest about my weakness. I am learning that to choose brave is to respond with faith and not fear, and to choose love and gratitude over worry and anxiety.

To embrace this bravery is simply to reject fear as the controlling force in my life. I turn to my Heavenly Father and say "yes" when He calls me deeper, confident that He supplies the grace I need for whatever He calls me to do, even if it feels scary. I simply embrace the bravery that is already mine.

Because being brave isn't about temperament or bravado. It is saying yes to the Spirit at work within me, changing the landscape of my mind, and bringing healing to the shattered places of my heart. The Spirit walks along side me and within me reminding me that the plans God has for me cannot be walked out in fear but rather in faith.

Can we sit here together for just a moment and try to imagine what it might look like - to live a life that is not ruled by insecurity? Close your eyes. Take a deep breath. Can you see it? It's okay if you can't even imagine it. I'm right here with you. I can only vaguely make out the shape of it in the distance. It can be hard to see. I'm much more familiar with the feeling of being un-brave.

Brave. What do you think about when you imagine the brave men and women of the Bible? Maybe you think about David facing Goliath, or Moses at the Red Sea. Maybe you picture Esther before the king, saving her nation from certain death. Maybe you think about Peter or Paul laying the foundation for the church. They were all amazing men and women and obviously brave characters in the unfolding story of God's redemption of His people. But during this study we're going to look at some of the more unexpected characters of the Bible who showed bravery in smaller, quieter ways.

Over the next few weeks we're going to look at the stories of Hannah - getting up out of her grief and surrendering her desires to God; Ruth - out in the fields choosing love in the mundane day after day after weary day; Hagar - who met God in the wilderness; Martha - who encountered Jesus in the middle of distraction; and her sister Mary - who sat at the feet of Jesus - giving us an example of what it looks like to see love responding to love. We're going to study characters who found bravery in weakness and at the very last bit of the end of their rope. Bravery that believes - despite everything we see - that God is still for us and we don't have to be afraid.

Writing this study has felt nothing like what I thought it was supposed to. It has not been written at a pretty desk in the rays of a rising golden sun, with a nice little stack of commentaries at my side, washed over by peace and joy. No way. This study feels like scribbled notes from the bomb shelter on the front lines of the battle against fear. It started as notes tapped out on my cell phone as I emptied the clothes dryer, and as I made dinner, and sitting on the edge of my tub, wrapped in a towel with tears streaming down my face.

To be totally honest - I have struggled with this - I have felt like my life should maybe feel more "together" and at least a lot less desperate if I'm going to write a Bible study on choosing brave. I have thought that someone who was actually brave should be writing about being brave, and not someone who was struggling to fight fear every single day. A few days later I felt God whisper that I am exactly where He wants me to be to write this. That my circumstances were not an overlooked detail of this plan, but exactly what He wanted. That He wanted me to write from this position, and from this posture and with this perspective. So here I am.

The format of this Bible Study is pretty simple. Each week there will be a simple story from the Bible and a couple of questions to ask God throughout the week. I'd suggest you sit with these questions as much as you can throughout the week. Ask them as a prayer and listen for how He leads. If you don't have the space in your life right now to do the homework (and we've all been there) no worries – we'll discuss the story and the response questions in our group meeting the following week. If you want to dig deeper, there are notes at the end of every week in the section "Background Study" to get you started.

My greatest desire for this study is that this would become a collection of moments when you met with God. May the Holy Spirit come and fill these pages with His words to you. This study has absolutely nothing to do with "right" answers, and everything to do with honest conversations with God. It's about coming to God barefaced and open-handed - with our jumbled tangle of thoughts and feelings - and letting Him set us right.

Discussion Questions :

What brings you to this Bible Study?

What do you think it means to be brave?

What do you think a brave person is like?

How does honesty about ourselves help us to embrace bravery?

What do you think it means to be brave in the quiet, everyday, ordinary moments of our lives?

What do you hope to get out of this study?

What then shall we say to these things?

If God is for us, who can be against us?

He who did not spare his own Son

but gave him up for us all,

how will he not also with him

graciously give us all things?

Romans 8:31-32 (ESV)

Week 1 Homework : Hannah

A while back, I was sitting in church listening to a sermon on Jesus' encounter with a man who had been sick for thirty-eight years. It is a story I have probably heard a hundred times. This time I was just not getting it.

You can find this story in John 5. It goes basically like this: Jesus approaches this man who is sick - a man who has possibly been sick for nearly his entire life - and they have this brief encounter that, on the surface, seems really strange to me. Jesus asks this guy "do you want to be healed?" and I could not get over how this felt like a really stupid question.

I know, I know. There are no stupid questions with Jesus. But it just didn't make any sense to me. What kind of a question is this to ask a sick man? Why would Jesus ask such an obvious question? It bothered me as I listened to the sermon. It bothered me as I drove home. It bothered me as I made lunch for my kids and it bothered me and bothered me until finally the Holy Spirit broke through and asked approximately the same question to me:

"What do you want?"

Just those simple words really hit me hard. It was a question that echoed in my soul for the next weeks. **"What do you want?"** I wondered - *"has my junk, heartache and issues so defined me that I can't imagine myself without them? Have I gone so far down this black hole of bitterness and resentment that I have given up on hope? Do I still believe that God is at work in my life? Do I still believe that He can do something amazing? Do I still want my broken heart, and broken life to be healed?"*

I found a lot of bravery in sitting with this question. It shaped my prayers over the coming months and helped to rally my faith during a moment when I really needed it. This is the question we are going to sit with as we begin this journey together: *"What do you want?"*

Let's sit here with Jesus. Face to face. He's not just asking a sick man by the pool. He's asking you: *"What do you want?"* Is there something that immediately comes to mind? With Jesus there are no *"but I've always been this way"* escape clauses. There is no temptation, no sin, no shame, no fear, no dream, no desire, no **anything** that is too big, too small or too hard for God.

In this moment it is really important to be honest. What do you *really* want? Not what you *should* want and not what you think other people expect you to want. Not what is safe enough to keep disappointment at bay, or feels like what is "reasonable".

Maybe you are thinking *"what does answering this question have to do with being brave?"* Here is my answer: because when we are living our lives with doors shut to desire we are living our lives with doors shut to God and who He made you and I to be. This was my first step: being honest about my own desires, my own pain, doubt and disappointment, and bringing them *honestly* to God.

Day 1 Hannah : Brave in My Disappointment

Today we're going to look at just the first bit of this story and watch as Hannah brings her grief to God. We'll consider how her response to God matches up with our own. As I began writing this study, this was the place where God asked me to begin. To be honest, it felt like a really weird place to begin. But it was the question I felt echoing in my soul. It turned out to be an invitation to explore some areas of deep disappointment, which had then resulted in deep doubt, which had given way to fear.

If you'd like to dig deeper into some of the background of this story you'll find some notes to get you started at the end of this week's homework.

Read: 1 Samuel 1:1-20

How does this text describe Hannah?

What is Hannah's relationship with her husband Elkanah like? (verse 5 & 8)

What is Hannah's relationship with her sister-wife Peninnah like? (verse 6-7)

Write out all of the words that describe Hannah's emotional state throughout this text:

The Amplified Version says that Hannah felt *"embarrassed and grieved"* about her childlessness.

These verses also say that her sister-wife Peninnah tortured her about it year after year. Every year, when the household traveled to Shiloh, Hannah was tortured for her childlessness, and every year she grieved - year after year after year.

Then one day, she does something different - she takes her grief and pours it out to God. Look back and re-read verses 7-9. As I was reading these verses again they hit me by surprise. She had been grieving about this year after year and then *finally* she gets up, goes to the temple and takes the desires of her heart to God. I'm over here like "I do this all of the time!!" I sit here crying about something (if only just in my heart), wishing for things to change but I'm just sitting here, wishing and crying and maybe texting my friends (hopefully not writing passive aggressive social media posts) but **what I need to**

do is get up and get into the presence of God. Hannah took her grief, her longing and her deepest desires and poured them all out to God.

It seemed like a humanly impossible situation, but God is bigger than that. He met Hannah in her impossible situation and did something amazing. (I want to be more like Hannah and be willing to ask God even for the things that seem impossible.)

What was Eli's initial impression of Hannah when he saw her in the temple?

Look at verses 15-17. The language in these verses is so poetic. Is there a phrase that jumps out to you in these verses? Here's mine: "*I have been pouring out my soul before the LORD.*" I just love this phrase.

God hears our prayers wherever we are, in fact sometimes I get my best prayer times in while I'm taking a shower or driving my minivan, however sometimes it is important for me to physically move. I need to get myself to church or Bible Study or small group. I need to ask my friends to pray for me, sometimes it's just over the phone but in some of my darkest moments, to have someone lay hands on me and pray for me has been the thing that kept me going. The most important thing isn't where or how or when. It's simply that we do.

What does God say about drawing near to Him?

Hebrews 4:16 & 10:19-23

Matthew 11:28-30

Ephesians 3:11-13

My dear friend, we cannot annoy God. God invites us to come. Over and over God invites us to simply come. Lets take God up on His offer: draw close, and linger there.

Reflect: Ask the Holy Spirit to help you look at yourself honestly - is there an area of your life where you have basically just been sitting and grieving instead of bringing it to God? Are you holding onto disappointment, or battling with doubt? What do you think is keeping you from bringing your desires fully to God? What is God saying to you about this?

Would you set down any anger, fear, pride, expectations, disappointment, or whatever you might call the heavy shield of armor that has kept you from feeling the big hard stuff? Will you just set it down, crawl up into the lap of your Daddy God and let it all out? All of the screaming, sobbing, messy parts that we try to keep hidden behind closed doors, and our "everything is okay" face.

Ask the Spririt to help you to be honest about your desires. Be bold and ask Him for the big, scary, crazy thing you have been too afraid to ask for. Pour out all of the small things that you've felt might be too trivial to bring to God. Open the door and let the wind of the Holy Spirit breathe new life into the dusty corners.

While you're in this moment spend some time listening. Usually when I am pouring out my heart to God, He is pouring His heart out to me too. What He has to say to each of us will be different but what He most often says to me is: "I'm here. I've got you. I won't let you go." I believe that in this moment you will hear God speaking into the deepest places of your own need. Take a few moments to journal your thoughts. Now is a good time - if you don't have one already, to ask a trustworthy friend to be your accountability partner and tell her about what God is showing you.

Write: What is one big question you are asking God today? What is one small thing you are asking God about today?

What is one moment this week when God showed up in your ordinary life?

Day 2 Hannah : Brave in My Surrender

Surrendering desire isn't just letting go of it - like loosing track of it, or pushing it way down deep where you can't see it in your day-to-day. It's not about secretly being angry or bitter about unfulfilled desires. Sometimes, to be honest, I don't want to hope. It has been so long, or it seems so unlikely, that I feel like I can't risk the disappointment. I can't risk the potential for feelings of failure. But here is what I'm learning: **when our hope is in God we will never be put to shame.** (Romans 5:5) Sure, things may not always turn out the way we thought they would, but when we put our hope in God we will ultimately not be disappointed.

Today let's sit here together to notice the full circle of this story. Hannah walked through month after month, year after year of disappointment. I purposefully left out the ending of this story in our earlier reading. Hannah's story doesn't end in 2:11.

Read: 1 Samuel 2:18-21

Hannah had this desire: to have a son. She gave her desire to God, God gave her the desires of her heart, she gave it back to God and God gave Hannah more children - both sons and daughters. Plural - more than one. Hannah asked God for "a son" and God gave her "sons and daughters".

Beside each statement write the reference for the verse that supports the statement:

Desire poured out to God _____

Desire surrendered to God _____

Desire fulfilled by God _____

Fulfilled desire devoted to God _____

Desire fulfilled even more abundantly by God _____

I want this to be something I know, not only as Hannah's story, but as my story too. I want to become, more and more, the kind of woman who brings her heart's desires fully to God. I want to be the kind of Jesus-follower who leaves it all in the loving, wise hands of my Heavenly Father, knowing that He'll give me what is best when the timing is right.

Reflect: What do you think is keeping you from bringing your desires fully to God? Are there areas of your life where your desire has become an idol? Are you struggling with unbelief? Are you holding out for a specific outcome? What do these verses have to say about bringing our desires to God?

A lot of these verses have to do with seeking God first. When our hope is in God first, and not in a specific outcome, we will not be disappointed. Write down any words or phrases that have to do with desire:
Matthew 6:33

Matthew 7:7-11

Ephesians 3:20

Romans 5:5

Write: Psalm 37:3-7 in your own words.

Background Study

"A certain man of Ramathaim-Zophim…": Also called Ramah. The name literally means "two watch towers". It was near Shiloh in the territory belonging to the half-tribe of Ephraim. (Joseph's tribe was devided into two half-tribes Ephraim & Manasseh). See: 1 Samuel 1:19, 1 Chronicles 6:66, Ruth 1:2, Joshua 18:21-28, 1 Samuel 2:11; 25:1. For more details look it up in Easton's Bible Dictionary on BibleHub.com.

Shiloh: This was the place of meeting for the whole community at the time of Samuel. This is where the tent of meeting was set up and where the priest lived. See: Deuteronomy 12:5-7, Joshua 18:1; 22:12.

"an Ephrathite": Someone who lived in the territory belonging to Ephraim who occupied a territory between Bethel & Shiloh, in the hilly area near Bethlehem (formerly called Ephrath). See: Genesis 41:50-52; 48:1-6, Joshua 16:5-10.

"and no razor shall touch his head": This was called the Nazarite vow. See: Numbers 6:1-5, Judges 13:1-7, Luke 1:5-17.

"Son of…": You know all of those lists of genealogies that we try not to yawn through? Here is where they get super-interesting. Samuel's family was in the lineage of Levi. The Levites were not given their own tribal lands when the Promised Land was divided between the tribes of Israel, the Levites were assigned to live with the other tribes. The Kohathites, descendants of Kohath, one of the sons of Levi, were assigned to live within the boundaries of the half-tribe of Ephraim and they were the keepers of the utensils of the inner-sanctuary. Kohath had a grandson named Korah and his descendants were called Korahites. In Numbers 3:11-13 Moses gave the law that every firstborn Levite was to be consecrated, or dedicated to the service of the temple. See: Genesis 29:34; 46:11, Exodus 6:16, 18, 21, 24, Numbers 3:27-32; 4:1-4, Joshua 21:1-5 & 20, 1 Chronicles 6:33-38, 66-70; 9:19-23.

"Sons of Korah": I don't tend to think of Samuel as a father or grandfather, or of how the context of his birth-family's heritage would have impacted his life or his future generations. He came from a family of Levites that served in the most sacred places of the temple. His grandson Heman was one of the principal singers in King David's choir next to Asaph & Ethan (or Jeduthun) and was one of the founders of the group "Sons of Korah" that are attributed as the writer of many of the Psalms. See: 1 Chronicles 9:19, Psalms 42, 87 & 88.

desire: It's a topic that sometimes gets a bad reputation. There are a lot of verses about deceitful desires and the "corrupted desires of our flesh." Sometimes we get so focused on those that we completely forget that our desires can also be a reflection of the image of God in us.

Questions for Reflection & Discussion : Week 1

Surrendering desire isn't just letting go of it, like loosing track of it, or pushing it way down deep where you can't see it in your day to day. It's not about secretly being angry or bitter about unfulfilled desires and it's not about chasing what you "ought" to desire. It's about honesty and trusting God to do what is best.

What do you think it means to be brave about our desires and disappointment?

Do you have a story of surrendering an outcome to God?

Where are you struggling with unbelief? How do you combat unbelief in your own life?

What are God's desires? How do I bring my desires into alignment with God's desires?

What big thing are you asking God for?

What small thing can you ask God about today?

What is one of the ordinary places where God has met you this week?

What verses help you most when you are struggling with unbelief? Bring one to share with your table group.

How precious is your steadfast love, O God!

The children of mankind

take regufe in the shadow of your wings

Pslam 36:7 (ESV)

Week 2 Homework : Ruth

There is a story in John 13, and it goes something like this: Jesus - nearing the end of his life, filled with love for his disciples and an awareness of his power and union with his Father - wanted to perform one last, grand gesture of love for his desciples. So He got up from the table, took off his jacket, and performed the task of the servant and washed their feet before the meal.

Hearing this story like this totally shifted how I thought about what it means to express love. That a "grand gesture of love" could mean going low and being the servant is on the one hand totally obvious, and yet on the other hand - when I think about what it means to be a servant in my home, and with my people - mind-blowing.

Because I totally get what it feels like to be the foot-washer, I know what it is like to spend all day doing the lowly, unnoticed, nothing thing, the un-appreciated, un-glamorous, un-respected thing. I know what it feels like to spend my life on what feels like nothing and yet in this space Jesus is teaching me that this nothing is really everything. Jesus chose to take the form of a servant. He chose to identify with the lowly, the unseen, the unheard, the un-chosen and He chose them. Jesus gave up splendor and He chose mundane.

> *"Have this mind among yourselves, which is yours in Christ Jesus, who, though he was in the form of God, did not count equality with God a thing to be grasped, but emptied himself, by taking the form of a servant, being born in the likeness of men."*
>
> **Philippians 2:5-7**

A few years ago my "word for the year" was *brave*. It felt like God was calling me out into the deep places with Him, where the waves were crashing and the water was deep. My circumstances were feeling equally intense and it made sense. So I started the year off with big requests for God - to take me deeper, to increase my faith and to help me learn what it means to live bravely. After a couple of weeks I felt like the tide went out and I was left standing in the mud. Knee-deep in ordinary life, slogging through homework and dishes, pregnancy hormones and pre-teen drama, up to my eyeballs in laundry, grocery shopping and overdue library books.

Looking back at that year I believe this season of "slogging through the mud" was more formative than I realized it was in the moment. In the moment it felt ordinary. Now, look-ing back, I see God was testing me to see if I would be faithful when the emotional high had passed and the tide of my feelings had gone out. I learned a lot about perseverance and about setting my face in the direction I felt God leading me and just moving forward in that direction trusting Him with the outcome, no matter my feelings.

This space of choosing mundane, this space of choosing love, and to love in the mundane - this is the space where He offers to exchange our fear (and my Cinderella complex) for something better. This is the space in which Jesus chose to demonstrate the full extent of His great love for His most special people. He is redeeming this space, the dirty and ordinary. He is saying *"this is how I love my people and this is how my people love."*

The Holy Spirit is fully engaged and active in even the most ordinary places of our lives, and through the work of the Spirit, is able to work even the most ordinary actions to achieve and extraordinary result.

Ruth is one of my heroes in the category of ordinary obedience. She took small steps of ordinary obedience that all led up to an extraordinary outcome and a mighty spiritual heritage. She was a woman of perseverance, faithful with the little and the lowly things but ultimately a precious mother in the linage of Jesus.

There are a couple of questions that come out of her story. One is this: do you believe that your everyday, ordinary acts of obedience have value? Here is another: where in your life are you experiencing low-grade fear? How can you replace fear with love?

Day 1 Ruth : Brave in My Mundane

It is so much easier for me to feel brave about a big hypothetical situation than it is to be brave about a real situation, even if it's relatively small. It is one thing to be brave on the mountaintop, to be brave walking on the water, or to be brave in the fire, to reach for faith in a moment of crisis. It is another thing altogether to be brave in the weary seasons of life.

Today we are going to begin our journey with Ruth. If you have the time today I'd recommend reading her whole story, from beginning to end, to get a big-picture overview of the whole thing, but if you're pressed for time just read the first chapter - that's where we'll be camping out during today's study.

Read: Ruth 1

As you read jot down any questions you have or general observations.

Be sure to pause after verse 5 and let the emotional impact of what you've read sink in. Can you even imagine what this must have felt like? My imagination can only scratch the surface of what this must have been like for them. Yes, **we know** that Ruth's story has a **happy ending, but she doesn't**. She's at a pretty dramatic low point in her story.

How does Naomi see God in relation to her suffering? (verse 13)

Verses 13 & 19-22 are really important for how we respond to difficult circumstances in our lives. Naomi blames God for her suffering and obviously feels that God has turned against her or is somehow punishing her, but we see at the end of verse 22 that God was still right there with them, providing for them, leading them towards a good future full of blessings. The fact that they arrive in Bethlehem at the beginning of the harvest meant that they wouldn't starve, because of the provision in the Jewish law for the poor that allowed them to glean in the fields during the harvests.

What do these verses say about suffering?
Psalm 34:18

Isaiah 54:10

1 Peter 1:3-9

James 1:2-4

Reflect: How does Ruth show bravery in the beginning of her journey?

How do you think bravery & love are related?

Is God calling you to persevere in a specific area?

How do you respond to God when life starts to feel more than a little bit crazy?

What is God saying to you about this?

How can you express love to those around you TODAY? Make a plan, tell your accountability partner, and then follow through!

Write a prayer confessing God's nearness in the chaos, weariness, and/or strait-up grief.

Day 2 Ruth : Brave in My Exhaustion

Last night I was up with my son. It was a miserable night with a sick kiddo who just wanted his mommy, while I just wanted to sleep. Last night as I sat there in the dark, barely awake, barely able to keep my frustration in check, and I thought about Ruth. I thought about her obedience and her faithfulness, and her bravery in ordinary things. I thought about how I don't usually think of these sleepless nights as requiring bravery or as being particularly spiritual. But down here in the mud of ordinary everyday obedience is actually where a ton of spiritual formation takes place. It's where the rubber meets the road, where you have to live out your intentions and practice what you preach. Whatever your "in the mud" place might be - school, office, kids, relationships - all of it can be used by God to refine us. **He can meet us in ordinary places, and work through ordinary actions to achieve an extraordinary story of His redemption.**

Read: Ruth 2-4

1:22 - harvest is beginning: _____

2:23 - harvest is ending:_____

One thing I noticed from the commentaries that I read about this text was that from the beginning of the barley harvest to the end of the wheat harvest would have been some- where around three months. Another thing I noticed was that at the end of the wheat harvest was a feast (the feast of booths or tabernacles) and in the instructions for this feast there is special reminder to provide for the servants, the travelers, Levites, orphans and - you guessed it - the widows (see Deuteronomy 16:14). There are also instructions about gleaning and care for the poor directly following the instructions for the harvest feasts. In a story that is all about how nothing is a coincidence, I don't think it is a coin- cidence that this story ends at this feast where the widow is remembered. Notice God's heart is towards these people in Deuteronomy 14:28-29.

Who takes the initiative? (verse 2):

How is Ruth described to Boaz? (verse 7):

What does Boaz offer Ruth? (verses 8-9) :

How would you describe Boaz? (see especially verses 14 & 16)

What is Naomi's reaction? (verse 19) :

How does Boaz describe Ruth? (3:11)

I love all of the dialogue in the book of Ruth. It not only moves the story along, but I think it shows a the culture in which this story is taking place, and the hearts of these people. One of the phrases we hear often in these chapters is the phrase "shadow of your wings" This metaphor is repeated again and again throughout scripture. Copy the phrases that stand out to you in the verses below:

Ruth 2:12

Ruth 3:9

Deuteronomy 32:10-12

Isaiah 51:16

Isaiah 59:21

Psalm 17:8

Psalm 57:1

Psalm 63:7

Psalm 91:1-4

Psalm 100:3

Remember at the beginning of the week, talking about Jesus's and the disciples. Did you notice Jesus' motivation for washing his disciples feet? Read John 13:1-5

Now do you notice what these verses say about fear and love? Read 1 John 4:18-19

Fear and love don't mix. They cannot cohabitate. In our middle spaces we are refined by our perseverance as we are motivated by love. We see the love between Ruth & Naomi and between Ruth & Boaz. They are different types of relationships but they are all active. In both sets of relationships they are actively looking out for the physical well-being of the other - the love that takes up the basin & towel.

Notice what these verses say about the steadfast love of God:

Psalm 31:1-3

Psalm 31:19-22

Psalm 36:5-10

Psalm 94:17-18

Isaiah 40:28-31

Reflect: How is Ruth's bravery blessed at the end of her story? What do you love about Ruth's ending? Can you think of a time when God blessed your obedience and the end of a season was marked by blessing? What are you believing about your own story? Are you stuck in a rut of worry and fear? How can you exchange that fear with love?

Write one of the verses above as a prayer:

Background Study

Moab: Abraham's nephew Lot is the father of the Moabites. God told the Israelites not to fight with the Moabites as they traveled through Canaan. See: Genesis 19:30-38 & Deuteronomy 2:1-9.

Gleaning: God's provision for the poor in the land. See: Deuteronomy 24:19-22, Leviticus 19:9-10, 23:22, Deuteronomy 14:29.

Kinsman-redeemer: This law kept property in the family, and was a provision for families that became poor. See: Leviticus 25:25. This is the law for the people of Israel for marriage to a widow. See: Deuteronomy 25:5-10. Also notice the connections between Ruth 4:11-12, & Genesis 38:6-11, 24-30.

Jesus' lineage: Ruth is one of the few women mentioned in Jesus' geneology. See: Ruth 4:18, Matthew 1:1-17.

Harvest Feasts: The harvest season - from the beginning of the barley harvest to end of the wheat harvest - was about three months. Barley harvest began right after Passover and the wheat harvest ended with The Feast of Weeks. The three major pilgrimage festivals in Judaism are Pesach (Passover) Shavout (Weeks) and Sukkot (Booths). Exodus 23:14-17, 34:18-21, Leviticus 23:4-43 (especially notice verse 22) , Numbers 28:16-29:12, Deuteronomy 16:1-17.

"Pesach" – The Feast of Unleavened Bread or Passover, is celebrated in the early spring (March or April) to remember the exodus of the Hebrews from Egypt.

"Shavout" – The Feast of Harvest, or the Feast of Weeks is celebrated at the beginning of the harvest (around June). It is celebrated fifty days after Passover (which is why it is also called the feast of Pentecost). The story of Ruth is traditionally read during the Feast of Weeks.

"Sukkot" – called the Feast Booths (or Tabernacles), also called the Feast of Ingathering is a week-long, joyful feast for giving thanks at the end of the year (around October) for the completion of the harvest.

Questions for Reflection & Discussion : Week 2

How do you relate to Ruth or Naomi in this story?

How do you think bravery & love are related?

How do you think bravery & perseverance are related?

What do you need to be brave about right now?

How do you respond to God when life starts to feel more than a little bit crazy?

Can you think of a time when God blessed your obedience and the end of a season?

How did you express love to people around you this week?

What did you learn (or remember) about God this week?

Why is this special/important to you right now?

What are some of the ordinary places that God has met you in this week?

The Lord will fulfill His purpose for me

your steadfast love, O LORD edures forever

Do not forsake the work of your hands

Psalm 128:8 (ESV)

Week 3 Homework : Hagar

Right now I am angry. More angry than I would ever like to admit – frustrated with my husband, about to loose my mind with my kids, I feel like a 5' 4" explosion waiting to happen and right this moment I feel like I can relate to Hagar. On the one hand, I find it impossible to relate to the details of Hagar's story - she was a foreigner, a slave, and eventually fled an abusive household - all things I cannot relate to even a little bit, but I can relate to the feeling of being in the wilderness.

Here are some words I have used when I felt in a wilderness:

- Scarcity
- Isolated
- Vulnerable (not in a good way)
- Loss of perspective
- Lack of direction
- Distracted
- Despairing

I might not have experienced what its like to be a slave or a foreigner or abused (maybe you do) but I know exactly what it is like to feel isolated and vulnerable. I know what it feels like to lack direction and focus. I know what it is like to wander around feeling at the end of my rope with no hope, and to feel invisible - like nobody hears me and nobody cares.

In these lonely places, when life feels altogether too much to handle, what I really need is for God to show up here with me. I need Him to be *El Roy* to me now - the God who sees me. When I fall face-first on the hot pavement of life, I need Him to come brush the gravel off of my knees, wipe the tears from my eyes and remind me that He'll never ever leave me. He will not fail me - not now, not ever.

At the end of the day, I'm amazed to notice the way God moves over and over to bless Hagar. Hagar wasn't looking for God, she was looking for a way out of her hard circum-stances, yet God showed up for her anyway. She had a pretty rotten attitude, and yet God was still faithful to her. The same God who rescued Hagar is my very own Daddy God who sees me even when I feel invisible.

This week we are going to ask God this question: where are you when I feel alone and unseen?

Day 1 Hagar : Brave When I Feel Invisible

Hagar was an Egyptian slave in Abraham & Sarah's household (she probably entered their household sometime around Genesis 12:16) but she did not appear to have a good relationship with Sarah. If you're not familiar with the story of Abraham & Sarah go ahead and consult the Background Study section of this week's homework. One important thing to note: Abram=Abraham & Sarai = Sarah. God changes their names a little later in this story.

Read: Genesis 16:1-16

About how many years had Abram & Sarai been waiting on children? (verse 3)

How old is Abram when Ishmael is born? (verse 16)

Why is Hagar in the wilderness? (verse 6)

Can we just pause here for a second to marvel in thankfulness that God is so faithful to His people - even when they walk themselves right on out into the wilderness. I have felt myself driven into the wilderness by the way others have sinned against me, but I've also foolishly taken my own self right on out into the wilderness - and God has met me there and been gracious to me.

What does the angel of the LORD tell her to do? (verse 9)

What does the angel say her son will be named? (verse 11)

Why is this his name? What does his name mean? (see the footnotes in your Bible or do a quick search online)

How does Hagar respond to this heavenly messenger? (verse 13)

What does she learn about God from this encounter?

Reflect: What words would you use to describe being in the wilderness?

Can you relate to feeling like you are in the wilderness?

Are you there currently? Have you been there recently? What is/was this like? How did you get there? How did/does it feel in the middle of it?

What are you afraid of?

But what is the truth?

What does it mean to you that God hears you?

What do these verses tell us about God's heart for us when we are in the wilderness?

Psalm 17:6-8

Psalm 61:1-4

Deuteronomy 1:30-31

Isaiah 51:3

What lies are you believing/have you believed about this wilderness season? This would be a good topic to discuss with your accountability partner.

What do you need to say to God today?

Write: Look up Psalm 84. Journal or write these verse in your own words as a prayer back to God.

Day 2 Hagar : Brave When I am Lost

Read: Genesis 21:9-19

It made me sad to read this story of Hagar, it's like she has completely forgotten her amazing experience with God when she was pregnant. She leaves Abraham and just wanders aimlessly in the wilderness. I kind of want to scream at her how could you forget!! Yet in the same breath I feel conviction because isn't that exactly what I do? I'm frustrated with this story because it doesn't end the way that I want it to end - it feels a little bit like Hagar took God's provision for granted.

Here is another moment to be reminded of why I love God and why He is so worthy of our trust & worship. When I am faithless He is faithful. He leads and guides even when I'm not listening or seeking Him. When I make a mess of everything He turns my ashes into something beautiful. He continues to be good to me again and again.

Read: Psalm 107

What has God rescued you from? Check each box that speaks to you.
- ❑ deserts
- ❑ darkness
- ❑ foolishness of sin
- ❑ storms

If you feel like you could check each box - me too! Depending on the day or the week or the year, I have wandered in the deserts of distraction and spiritual dryness. I have sat in the darkness of depression and hopelessness. I have chased the foolishness of sin, and I have certainly weathered a storm or two - I'm guessing you have too.

Look up the following verses. If you're running short on time you can look up the verses for the categories that speak most to you.

What does God do for us who wander in the **deserts**? (Isaiah 35:1-10, John 7:37-39)

What does God do for us who sit in the **darkness**? (Micah7:7-9, Isaiah 9:2, John 8:12)

How does God respond to us who are **sinning**? (Isaiah 42:3-7, Deuteronomy 8:2-16)

How does God act for us who are in the middle of the **storms**? (Isaiah 54:10-14 & 43:2)

Write: How has God rescued you?

How is God meeting you in the lonely places of your life right now?

Additional Verses:

Deuteronomy 31:6, 8

1 Chronicles 28:20-21
(look it up in The Message Translation)

Psalm 20:5

Psalm 27:4-6

Psalm 34:1-5

Psalm 37:23-24

Psalm 95:1-2

Isaiah 33:6

Isaiah 40:11

Isaiah 54:1-14

Isaiah 58:11-12

Ezekiel 34:26-31

Luke 12:13-34

Romans 16:25-27

1 Corinthians 1:26

Philippians 4:4-7

Background Study

If you don't know the story of Abraham and Sarah, here is the short version: God made a covenant promise to Abraham (when his name was Abram) that he would become the father of a nation (Genesis 12:1-5, 15:1-6). The only problem was that he and his wife Sarah (at the time named Sarai) were having fertility issues (Genesis 17:15-20). Abraham and Sarah struggled mightily to believe that God would be faithful to them, and made all kinds of idiotic choices - lying to neighboring kings about Sarah's relationship with Abraham, (Genesis 12:10-20, & 20:1-7) and using a concubine to conceive an heir (Genesis 16) and yet God was faithful and through a miracle Sarah did eventually conceive a son (Genesis 21:1-3) who was named Isaac, who became the father of Jacob (Genesis 25:19-28), who was later re-named Israel (Genesis 35:9-15).

Wilderness: Jesus often withdrew to the wilderness to have time with God. Jesus used the wilderness as a tool for spiritual formation. Matthew 4:1, Mark 1:12-13, 3:7 & 13, 4:13-14, 6:30-32 & 45-47. See also: Hebrews 2:18, 4:15, Hosea 2:14.

Questions for Reflection & Discussion : Week 3

How do you relate to Hagar in this story?

How does God respond to Hagar?

Do you relate to being in a wilderness season?

What was that like?

> What were you afraid of?

> How did you respond to God in this season?

> What did you learn about God through that season?

What did you learn/remember about God this week?

Why is this special/important to you right now?

What do you need to be brave about right now?

How is God calling you, specifically, to act out your brave?

What are some of the ordinary moments that God has met you this week?

To the thirsty I will give

from the spring of the water of life

without payment.

Revelation 21:6 (ESV)

The water that I will give

will become a spring of water

welling up to eternal life

John 4:14 (ESV)

Week 4 Homework : Martha & Mary

Let me tell you what - writing this particular part of this study during this particular week could not be better timing. I think I lost my mind sometime last week and if there was ever a time when I felt like I absolutely don't have the time or the mental focus to be working on this study - it is now. I feel Distracted — with a capital D.

For the next two weeks we will be looking at four stories about two sisters. Both sisters are present in each story but this week we are going to focus on Martha and next week we'll be focusing on her sister Mary. The stories of Martha & Mary remind me very much of a story Jesus told (you can read it in Luke 15:11-30) it's often called "the parable of the prodigal son".

In this parable there is a father and his two sons. The younger son asks to receive his inheritance, he is given it, and then he travels far away. The ESV translation says he squandered all his money "in reckless living." Then there was a famine in the country where he was living - like a recession in the economy - and the only work he could find was out feeding pigs. Suddenly he comes to his senses, realizes that even the servants in his father's house are treated better than what he is experiencing, and he decides to head back home.

Along the way he prepares this speech about how he has sinned, and how he is not worthy of being called a son, and he plans to beg his father to just give him a job. But his father spots him before he even gets close to the house and runs out to meet him. The father embraces the son, welcomes him, invites him in, and celebrates his return.

The older son, who was out in the fields working when all of this happened, comes to the house at the end of the day. When he hears the music and the noise from the party, he asks one of the servants *"what's going on?"* When he hears about what has gone down with his younger brother - how he'd returned and how his father was throwing a feast for him - the older son gets angry. His father comes out and tries to persuade his older son to come in and join the feast, but his son makes this angry, bitter speech. He says *"look at how many years I have served you, without ever disobeying a single command, and you never gave me anything to celebrate with my friends! But this son of yours, who wasted your money on prostitutes, you threw a huge party for him!"* You can almost hear the *"that's not fair!"* at the end of his speech.

His father says *"Son, you are always with me, and everything that is mine is yours. It is right for us to celebrate and be happy because your brother was dead, but now he is alive, he was lost and now he is found."*

The story is about the foolish younger brother and it is about the older brother, the obedient, responsible one, but it is mostly about God, the father in this story. The word "prodigal" can mean a person who spends money in a recklessly, extravagant way. It comes from the Latin word *prodigus* meaning "lavish" but it can also mean having or giving something on a lavish scale to the point of being wasteful, generous, unsparing, unrestrained, bountiful.

This story has also been called the story of the prodigal father because while it is a story about the younger son's reckless spending it is also the story of the father's reckless love. It is a story about a father's lavish forgiveness, and extravagant grace. It's also a warning exposing the ugliness of our unwillingness to receive or extend grace. I want you to keep this love in the back of your mind as you read these stories.

Day 1 Martha : Brave in My Distraction

If you have been in church, especially in Women's Bible Studies, for very long you have probably heard about these sisters. It's such a common story that it has become a cliché. Sometimes I feel like these sisters are misrepresented, other times I feel like they are over-spiritualized. As you read these verses ask the Holy Spirit to speak to your spirit the words you need to hear, and to open the eyes of your heart to see the things about yourself that you need to see.

Read: Luke 10:38-42

What is Martha doing?

What is her sister Mary doing?

It's worth noting that this was highly unusual. What Mary is doing in this story is outside of her cultural norm. Women in their culture were not often welcome to sit at the feet of a teacher as a student. Women and girls were expected to stay busy serving in the home.

How do you think Martha is feeling in this moment?

In my translation it reads that Martha was "distracted with much serving". I was going to ask you to write down a time when you felt this way but I was thinking we would all pretty much answer, "um, like five minutes ago?!" Can you relate to this?

Who did Martha blame for how she was feeling? (verse 40)

I feel the sting of conviction in this question, because I can be such a blamer. I notice that I tend to blame whoever is closest to me, or I take out my frustration on the nearest person who I think won't hurt me back - like my husband, and especially my kids. Who do you tend to blame for feeling overwhelmed, distracted or generally all over the place?

What does Jesus say to Martha? (verse 41)

Reflect: How have you experienced a season of distraction?

What was distracting you?

How did you feel in general during that season?

What are the distracted places in your life right now?

How can you reclaim some of these distracted places in your day?

When can you get quiet and rest in the middle of your busy life?

What do you do when you are choosing to rest?

Sometimes I will try to take a nap, draw a bath, make myself a cup of tea or get out my journal. Other times the most spiritually restful thing I can do at the end of the day is take a walk alone. What is one way you can commit to guarding some space to sit at the feet of Jesus? Talk to your accountability partner about your plan.

Write down any words or phrases that stand out to you:

Matthew 11:28-30 in a standard translation:

in the Amplified version:

in The Message translation:

Day 2 Martha : Brave in My Gifting

I love these two sisters. Mary, so wild and emotional, while Martha seems to me like a type-A, task-oriented, rule-follower. These two sisters could not be more different but through these two encounters (and two more next week) we see that Jesus loves both of them. I love that Martha wasn't defined by a single moment and that she didn't freak out *every time* she had people over. I love this story *so much* because even though Martha only gets a few words in this story - they are powerful, redemptive words.

Read: John 12:1-8

Notice in verse 2 - what does it say about Martha? What is she doing?

Did you notice? It's the exact same thing she was doing in the story we looked at yesterday. She is exercising her gift of hospitality, serving Jesus and his disciples (and every other person who wandered into this dinner party) and providing the backdrop to this moment with Jesus. She was exercising her gifting, and using her strengths for the good of God's kingdom coming. It can be tempting when we have messed up or embarrassed ourselves to want to hide our light.

Reflect: Have you ever had a moment when you stepped out and then fell on your face? Do you know what your spiritual gifts are? You probably have more than one. You can easily look up a spiritual gifts survey online, or ask your pastoral staff about which one they recommend. However, the best way to learn about your spiritual gifting is to simply jump in and serve where it is needed and listen to the feedback you receive. You'll learn - through trial and error - where you are most gifted.

Write your thoughts and observations about spiritual gifting in these passages:
Romans 12:3-10

1 Corinthians 12:4-7, 12-2

Ephesians 4:11-16

Side note: As I was researching this I noticed how many times these lists of gifting and discussions of the various strengths and apparent weaknesses within the church end on a note of love! 1 Corinthians 12 is about gifting and chapter 13 is the most famous chapter about love. Serving with love is important work - it is beautiful, and so valuable.

Background Study

Bethany: Matthew 21:17, Mark 11:1, 11-12,
John 11:1 – Lazarus, Martha & Mary in Bethany
John 12:1-8 – Mary anoints Jesus at Bethany
Luke 24:50 - Jesus led the disciples to Bethany

In the commentaries I read about the city of Bethany one of the things that was mentioned is that this place was possibly somewhere where sick were taken care of, just outside of Jerusalem, and a place where the extrememly poor slept.

Jesus says to Martha "you are anxious and troubled about many things". Here are a few verses that speak to anxiety Luke 12:22-34, Matthew 6:25-34; 7:7-11

I want to take a moment here to talk about anxiety. Sometimes in church we talk about anxiety like it is something we can just pray away. Like, if we just had enough faith or believed all the right things about God then we would no longer experience any anxiety. This is unhelpful because it creates an atmosphere of shame around anxiety. There is another mentality I've noticed around anxiety though, and that is to play the role of victim. Like we are saying *this is just the way I am. There is nothing I can do about it. I just have to live with my anxiety.* I've noticed that both mentalities are unhelpful because the first one makes us feel that our anxiety is a sin and that if we just had enough faith we would not struggle with it and that's not true. The other makes it seem like this is just the way we are and there is nothing we can do about it and that's not true either. There is a sweet spot in the middle, I think - a place where **God wants to meet us in our anxiety** and sit with us, and still our anxious hearts and busy minds with His truth.

Questions for Reflection & Discussion : Week 4

How do you relate to Martha this week?

How do you think choosing brave and choosing rest work together?

How can you reclaim some of these distracted places in your day?

When can you get quiet and rest in the middle of your busy life?

What do you do when you are choosing to rest?

What is one way you can commit to guarding some space to sit at the feet of Jesus?

Have you ever had a moment when you stepped out and then fell on your face?

Do you know what your spiritual gifts are?

What did you learn (or were reminded) about God this week?

Why is that important to you right now?

How did God meet you this week?

But we have this treasure in jars of clay

to show that the surpassing power

belongs to God and not to us

2 Corinthians 4:7 (ESV)

Week 5 Homework : Mary & Martha

I don't often feel God leading me in the area of organization, but I was sitting in Panera in a rare moment away from my family to write, sketching out the last few weeks of this study I felt like God wanted this week to be the note to go out on. I felt like at the end of this study God wanted you to be left with only one thing:

"I love you."

It is tempting, especially if we have been trapped under the glass ceiling of shame, to think we need to do and do and do in order to be loved. But God is calling us, ever so tenderly, to drop that lie and embrace the truth that you and I are already loved and the only kind of obedience that He wants from us is love responding to love.

This week we are going to peek into two moments with Mary & Martha. The first moment is recorded in all four of the gospels. I've given you the references in my background study notes, each story shares slightly different details.

Day 1 Mary : Brave in My Shame

I still remember the day when God invited me to break through the glass ceiling of how close I could get to him. I had been living in a cloud of shame for the last few years. I was a former-front-row "Good Christian" who had been hanging out on the back row, doubting, disbelieving and even at times disobeying God. I felt like a failure - one of "those" people who don't really belong, someone who "should have known better." But it was in this place, during my stint on the back-row, that God showed me that there was no distinction in His heart, no "us" and "them" within His body, only His children, dearly loved ones.

Living in shame about our past is one of the enemy's go-to moves in his plan to keep us powerless and ineffective. You can't fully be the person that God created you to be if you are living in the shame of your past.

We read a version of this story last week, and in our background study we looked at the four parallel texts for this encounter with Jesus. Today we are going to read this version of the story. In this version of the story the woman is unnamed, but looking at the parallel stories it is most likely that the woman in this story is Martha's sister Mary.

Read: Luke 7:36-50

What did Simon say about her?

What didJesus say to her?

Mary *clearly* understood her sin, and everyone around her seemed to know about it too, and yet she drew near with an act of love and worship that was as extravagant as the forgiveness she had recieved.

Regardless of if you have managed to keep the façade of respectability in-tact or not, if your failures have been public or private, I am guessing that at some point you have had to come face to face with the dark corners of your heart. God brought me through a season of revealing the darkness in my heart a few years ago. I got a front row seat, and a backstage pass to see my own sin. My sin and temptations are not something vague anymore, and Satan loves to throw them back up into my face.

I remember one of the moments when I realized how far I had wandered away from God. One day of distraction had piled on top of the next one and before I knew it the path of blessing was miles away and I was neck-deep in my own mess. In this moment I was face-down on my bedroom floor screaming out to God "how could you let me wander this far away?!!!" And in that moment I clearly heard the Holy Spirit whisper in my spirit "so that you would know this." And in my spirit I felt God sweep me up in His loving arms and surround me with his presence and His unfailing, unshakeable love. It was one of the most powerful intense moments of my walk with God.

What do you see about God's hear for you in these verses?

John 14:15-24

Romans 5:5

Joel 2:25-27

Isaiah 61:7

Galatians 5:16-17

We are imperfect, but we are *perfectly* loved.

*"This is the way GOD put it: "They found grace out in the desert, these people who survived the killing. Israel, out looking for a place to rest, **met God out looking for them!"** **GOD told them, "I've never quit loving you and never will. Expect love, love, and more** **love!**..." Jeremiah 31:2-6 MSG*

How do I respond to such love? With more wandering? More distraction? More laziness? More sin?

"No test or temptation that comes your way is beyond the course of what others have had to face. All you need to remember is that God will never let you down; he'll never let you be pushed past your limit; he'll always be there to help you come through it." 1 Corinthians 10:13 MSG.

"Well then, should we keep on sinning so that God can show us more and more of his wonderful grace? Of course not! Since we have died to sin, how can we continue to live in it?" Romans 6:1-2 NLT

I respond to love with love.
"This is real love—not that we loved God, but that he loved us and sent his Son as a sacrifice to take away our sins. Dear friends, since God loved us that much, we surely ought to love each other. No one has ever seen God. But if we love each other, God lives in us, and his love is brought to full expression in us." 1 John 4:10-12 NLT

When we realize how much God loves us all we have left to do is love Him back. If we love Him - we keep His commands, we follow in His paths, we delight in what He delights in, and we hate what He hates, the Spirit fulfills the law of love from within.

What is your glass ceiling? Is there something separating you from getting really close to God? It may be in your past, or it may be in your present. It might seem like something big or something small - our accuser will throw anything at us he thinks will stick. Hear me loud and clear. The separation is only in your own mind. God's heart for you is to be close.

Always.

P.S. I just want to offer a note to you who are reading this and identify more with Simon than with the sinful woman. You have kept your stuff together. You've been obedient. Maybe you know exactly what Jesus means when he tells Simon that he has been forgiven little. I have certainly sat in that place many many times. Here are the verses that I wanted to share with you sweet sister. Turn the page back one or two to Luke 6:37-38. In my translation the words I have underlined are these "with the measure you use it will be measured back to you."

I want to be given a generous measurement - given the benefit of the doubt, looked at with the eyes of love. It is not calling for a lack of discernment but this is a reminder to not fall into the trap of being judgmental. To not judge ourselves, or other people, too harshly. I find myself ping-ponging between feeling smothered by shame and being judgmental towards others. The sweet spot where I want to live is where I practice discernment with a heavy dose of love. Learning how God sees me, and then looking at others in the same way as much as I am able. I am learning how to practice grace and forbearance, love and mercy for myself and for others. See also: John 3:16-21 & James 2:13, Matthew 18:21-35, Colossians 3:12-14

Day 2 Mary : Brave in a Crisis

This morning I drove home from the Emergency Room and cried as I turned off the radio. I wanted to scream at the steering wheel, instead I just drove and cried quietly in the silence. My husband asked "what are you thinking?" and I just said "I thought things were getting better." Until today I had been feeling like this roller coaster down had hit the bottom and we were heading up again. I thought things were going to get better. But now, all over again, I feel at the end of my rope. Hanging on by a thread.

Sometimes when I go through things in life I just brace. I try to wait it out, and rush through. However what I am learning, as I weather the storms of life, is to learn to go through pain with an open heart, and to let the pain it do its good work. I am learning to be actively engaged in choosing hope.

Like a birth, I don't lie there passively, waiting for this to be over. I am actively controlling my breathing, actively choosing to relax my body, believing that this season of difficulty will birth something beautiful. I don't want to fight against the labor pains. If I get tense and fight against the pain, then my labor will stall.

During hard times too. I am present in the middle of this pain and I am chasing hope with everything I've got, clinging to the truth of God's presence here with me with all my might, fighting fear with every ounce of power within me, reminding myself over and over and over and over that God is good. He will not abandon me, He will never ever fail me.

I choose bravery by being open about the pain, not just letting it spill out on whoever is nearby but purposefully choosing to share my life and allowing others to help me. I plant both of my feet into God, my rock. I keep my eye on the horizon, confident that He will work something beautiful out of this set of hard circumstances.

Martha and her sister Mary faced their own personal crisis, the death of their brother. They responded in different ways and Jesus loved them both.

Read: John 11:1-44

Who sent a message to Jesus? (verse 3)

What does the message say? "_____is sick"

What does Jesus say is the purpose of this sickness? (vesrse 4)

What do you think this means?

Look at verse 5 and also verse 36 – what do these verses say about Jesus' relationship with these siblings?

What does Jesus do as a result of the answer to the above? (verse 6)

Why does the disciple Thomas say in v 16 "let us also go?" What was the mood around Jesus at this time? (hint: John 10:19, 31, 39)

Lazarus has been dead for _____ days. (verse 17)

William Hendrickson's commentary says:
"According to rabbinical tradition, the soul of a deceased person hovers around the body for three days in hope of a reunion, but takes its final departure when it notices that the body has entered a state of decomposition."

How many days did the soul hover near the body? _____ days.

Who went to go see Jesus first? (verse 20) How did she respond to Jesus?

What does Jesus say to her? "I am _____."

What question does Jesus ask in verse 26?

What is similar/different about Mary & Martha's encounters with Jesus? (verses 20-21, 32-33)

How does Jesus respond to them? (vers 35)

What do the people around Jesus & Mary say? (verse 37)

What does Martha say when Jesus says to take away the stone? (verse 39)

What happens next?

Jesus said that **this death was to bring glory to the Son of God.** To be honest this idea of sorrow and pain, and especially premature death as "glorifying God" is hard for me to understand. It's a phrase I hear quite a lot in church, from people who maybe don't know what else to day. When my brother died when he was only 16 years old I heard this a lot, even from my own family, and it just made me want to scream. I wanted to weep with Mary "where were you when my brother died?" and I wanted to murmur with the crowds "couldn't he have prevented this?"

In Isaiah 49:3 it says "You are my servant, in whom *I will be glorified*" and the alternate text in my Bible says "or I will display my beauty" and these words have shifted how I think about "glorifying God" I think about it more as displaying God's beauty, or in other words, something that is true about God. So as Jesus waited with purpose and arrived after it was reasonable to hope, he did so in order to display something that was true about God and true of himself as the Son of God.

Here is another thing I noticed: according to their tradition, the soul of the departed hovered near the body for three days, but Jesus showed up on the fourth day. The sisters sent a message to Jesus, and I am guessing they must have been full of hope that he would come and heal their brother, but Jesus waited. After their brother died they might have still hoped he would come in a day or two and resurrect their brother, but still they waited for Jesus to show up, and by the fourth day the hope would be pretty much gone.

It was an impossible thing to hope that Jesus would raise their brother from the dead, a totally unreasonable expectation. Here is a truth I am learning, one that we looked at in week 1 of our study: even when it seems unreasonable to hope, hope in God will never put me to shame (see Romans 5:5) When Jesus showed up, at the right time for HIS plan, not theirs, he did the impossible.

Reflect: Have you experienced moments when you could have said, along with the crowd: "I thought you loved me? Couldn't you have kept this from happening?

Is there anything in your life that feels beyond hope, like past the time when it would be reasonable to expect a resurrection?

There's honestly a lot I don't understand about this story. I don't understand why, when Jesus knew that he'd come to raise Lazarus, he chose to pause and weep here with Mary. I don't understand it, but I love him so much for this. I love that Jesus shows us that God stops to weep with us when we are weeping.

Write a prayer to God:

_____, the one you love....
          (write your name here)

Background Study

Today we are going to compare the four accounts of this one encounter with Jesus. There is some variation in the stories, this is to be expected, notice the differences, but focus on the similarities. As you read this same story four times let it be like adding layers, each layer adds to the beauty and richness of this experience that Jesus had with his friend. Note the details of these encounters: who is in this story, how are they described, where does this encounter take place, what happen. Also pause to journal any thoughts that come to mind as you read about this encounter with Jesus.

Luke 7:36-50 – Jesus anointed

Matthew 26:6-16 – Jesus anointed at Bethany

Mark 14:3-11 – Jesus anointed at Bethany

John 12:1-8 – Jesus anointed by Mary at Bethany

How Jesus responded to other women:

John 4:1-42 – Samaritan woman

John 8:1-11 – woman caught in adultery

Mark 5:25-34 & Luke 8:43-48 – Jesus heals a bleeding woman

John 20:11-18 – Jesus appears to women after the resurrection

Wrap-up Questions

Think about how you typically respond to crisis - do you relate most Mary or Martha?

What did you learn/remember about God this week?

Why is this special/important to you right now?

Did you have a favorite character in this study?

How does honesty about ourselves help us to embrace bravery?

How do you think perserverance helps us to embrace bravery? '

What do you think a brave person is like?

How did God meet you in this study?

Leader Guide

As you work through the material remember that the point of these sessions is to encounter God in our questions. So as we lead our discussion groups we want to lead with questions. Here are my suggestion for how to go through the material so that you can be prepared:

Day 1 - Read the main texts for the week and go over the notes for Background Study. Make notes, ask questions, & follow your curiosity. Use web resourses like Bible.com, BibleHub.com, StudyLight.org, BlueLetterBible.org, & BibleGateway.com to help get more information. It wouldn't hurt to quickly look over the questions for reflection & discussion so you can begin to turn the questions over in your mind as you go through the week.

Day 2 - Complete homework for Day 1. The homework days are days to recieve and be filled up. Try to approach your homework days as a student, with humility and honesty. If your "leader brain" kicks in write a note and move on.

Day 3 - Complete homework for Day 2. This would be a good day to reach out to your group and connect with them mid-week.

Day 4 - Look through Questions for Reflection & Discussion and answer them for yourself. Journal your responses.

Day 5 - Prepare for the meeting. Look over your notes from the preceding days, pick 4 questions to focus on during discussion time.

Made in the USA
Middletown, DE
17 April 2023

28989098R00031